Outline Stickers

D1089402

*Dedicated to my daughter
Ruthie and Ashley my
son-in-law... the new Mr
and Mrs Powell!*

Outline Stickers

Judy Balchin

SEARCH PRESS

First published in Great Britain 2006

Search Press Limited
Wellwood, North Farm Road,
Tunbridge Wells, Kent TN2 3DR

Text copyright © Judy Balchin 2006

Photographs by Roddy Paine Photographic Studios

Photographs and design copyright © Search Press Ltd. 2006

ISBN 1 84448 103 4

Suppliers

If you have difficulty in obtaining any of the materials and
equipment mentioned in this book, then please visit the Search
Press website for details of suppliers: www.searchpress.com

> **Publisher's note**
>
> All the step-by-step photographs in this book feature the
> author, Judy Balchin, demonstrating how to use outline stickers.
> No models have been used.

Manufactured by Universal Graphics Pte Ltd, Singapore
Printed in Malaysia by Times Offset (M) Sdn Bhd

Acknowledgements

A big thank-you goes to Norbert Verbeek
of Audenaerde Creative and to
Andrew Knoles of Do Crafts for
supplying the majority of the outline
stickers used in this book.

Very special thanks go to the ever-friendly
team at Search Press for their continued
support. In particular, Roz Dace for her
expert guidance, editor Edward Ralph for
his humour and energy, Juan Hayward for
his wonderful design skills, and Roddy
Paine for his stylish photography.

I would like to thank Ruthie and Ashley
Powell, my daughter and son-in-law, for
allowing me to use their beautiful wedding
photographs in the book.

Thanks to Daisy Nella and her parents
John and Louise for letting me use
their photographs.

Page 1: Tulip card

*The outline sticker is pressed on to acetate
and decorated with fine glitters.*

Page 2: Cherub plaque

*The stickers are pressed on to white card and
coloured with crayons. They are then cut out
and mounted on top of each other to create
the three-dimensional effect.*

Page 3: Snowman box

*Outline stickers are painted with acrylic paints
and pressed on to a sponge-painted box.*

Opposite: Floral glitter card

*Glitter and marker pens are used to decorate
the larger floral sticker. Marker pens are used
to colour the smaller stickers.*

Contents

Introduction

Welcome to the world of the outline sticker. If you have not used them before you are in for a real treat; and even if you have this book will inspire you to 'carry on sticking'!

Outline stickers are inexpensive, easy to use and fun. They make cardmaking, scrapbooking and decoration a sheer pleasure and take all the hard work out of crafting. The sticker sheets contain dozens of motifs covering all themes so you will have no trouble finding one to suit your needs. You can choose from sheets of animals, flowers and figures and also a wealth of borders, frames and lettering. My biggest problem in writing this book was choosing just which outline stickers to use!

I am often amazed at what effects can be produced with just a humble sticker or two. Using interesting backing papers and card with a few extra embellishments can produce very professional results indeed. The techniques used in this book are simple and fun to do. Mounting and layering, painting and colouring the stickers, glitter decoration, embossing and three-dimensional papercraft are all covered, plus a lot more. Whether you want to make a birthday or Christmas card; create a scrapbook or bookmark; decorate a gift box, picture frame or book cover, this book is for you.

Having read this introduction, you may be wondering what to do next. My advice is to flip through the pages until something takes your fancy... and have a go! Happy sticking!

Judy.

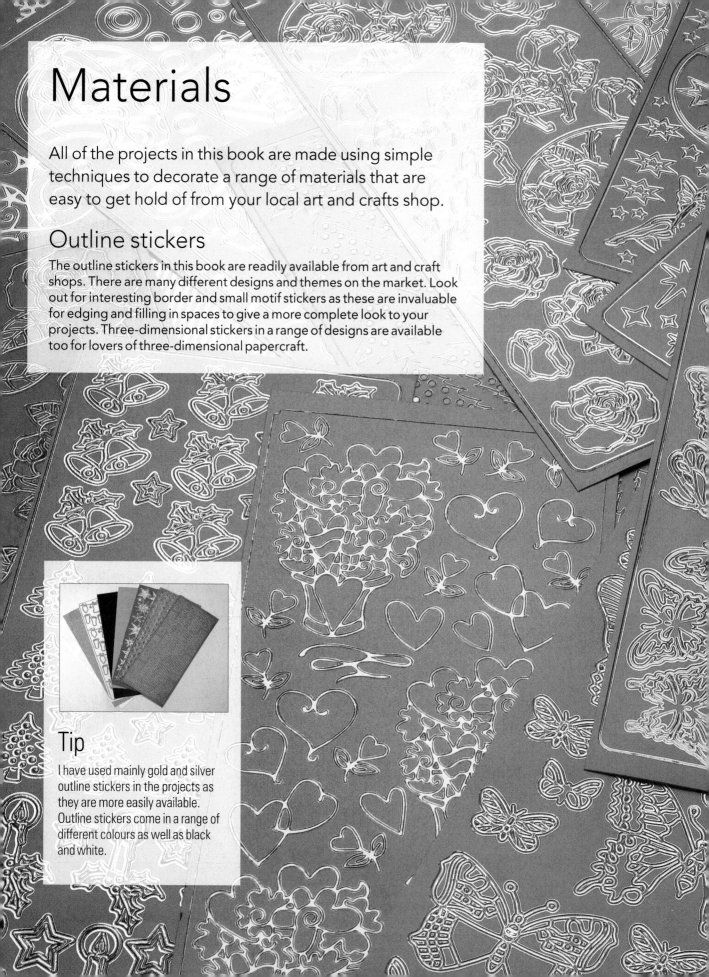

Materials

All of the projects in this book are made using simple techniques to decorate a range of materials that are easy to get hold of from your local art and crafts shop.

Outline stickers

The outline stickers in this book are readily available from art and craft shops. There are many different designs and themes on the market. Look out for interesting border and small motif stickers as these are invaluable for edging and filling in spaces to give a more complete look to your projects. Three-dimensional stickers in a range of designs are available too for lovers of three-dimensional papercraft.

Tip

I have used mainly gold and silver outline stickers in the projects as they are more easily available. Outline stickers come in a range of different colours as well as black and white.

Backing materials

These are what make your projects work really well. There is a huge array of cards and papers in many different colours available in art and craft shops. This selection includes handmade papers, metallic and glitter card, corrugated card, patterned background papers, lettered vellum, webbing, metal embossing foils and acetate.

Tip

Photographs can be used as backgrounds, or used for scrapbooking projects.

Blanks

Look out for papier-mâché boxes and frames in unusual shapes. Blank albums and notebooks are also available in art and craft shops.

Embellishments

Sequins, craft jewels, ribbons, raffia, wire and embroidery threads are all used as embellishments throughout the book. Fine glitter is used with glue and acetate to decorate stickers. Glitter glue is also available.

Paints, pens and crayons

Glass paints can be used to paint stickers mounted on acetate. Gouache, acrylic paints and coloured crayons are used to colour stickers when mounted on to card. Use acrylic paint to colour blanks before decorating with stickers. Marker pens can also be used to colour the outline stickers and there is a range of pens designed specifically for this purpose.

It is easiest to use these pens while the sticker is on the backing sheet. Due to the stickers' glossy surface, the ink will not dry immediately, so you can even blend two colours together by using a different marker pen on top of wet ink. Once you are happy with the colours, leave them to dry for a few seconds, and be careful not to smudge the ink as you lift the sticker off the backing sheet.

Other materials

Pencil Use this to draw lines and trace round templates.

Paintbrushes Used for painting outline stickers with gouache or acrylic paints. Use a soft paintbrush to brush away glitter particles.

Palette Use this to mix paint and when applying paint to a blank item with a sponge.

Sponge Use a piece of inexpensive sponge to dab paint on to a surface.

Ruler Use to measure and draw straight lines or with the back of a scalpel to score card ready for folding.

Scalpel Use this to lift the outline stickers, to cut and score card on a cutting mat and to cut out stickers mounted on card.

Cutting mat Use this when trimming stickers or cutting card with a scalpel.

Scissors Round-ended scissors are used for cutting thin card and paper, and also for pushing the spine flap into place when covering a book.

Old notepad This is placed under the foil when embossing work is being done.

Old scissors Use these to cut wire.

Masking tape Use this for securing acetate before painting and for taping it to a card before assembling.

Ballpoint pen To be used for embossing work.

Double-sided sticky pads Larger pads are used to attach stickered panels to a base card to give a three-dimensional effect. Smaller pads are used to mount the three-dimensional outline stickers on top of each other.

Spray adhesive Use this to fix backing paper on to card.

Strong clear adhesive This is used to glue metal foil to a surface and to attach craft jewels.

White glue fitted with a fine nozzle This dries clear and is used to decorate sticker panels with glitter. The metal nozzle is bought separately and screwed on to the glue bottle.

Hole cutting tool, hammer and mat Use these for punching holes in the Christmas decoration and gift tags.

Cotton buds Cotton buds are used for bringing out fine details when embossing.

Christmas Card

Simple outline stickers can be used to great effect when combined with unusual backing card and a few extra embellishments.

In this project, the texture of the corrugated card contrasts well with the gold decoration to give a really sophisticated look. Spirals of wire and gold thread can easily be attached by trapping them between the sticker and the card with double-sided sticky pads, so giving an added sparkle to your festive creation.

The stickers used in this project.

1. Lift the star sticker from the backing sheet with the tip of a scalpel.

2. Place it on the gold card and press it flat with your fingers.

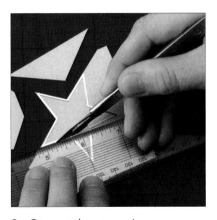

3. Cut out the star using the scalpel.

4. Press the heart sticker on to the card and cut it out. Cut a sticky pad to fit the back of the heart decoration and peel off the backing paper.

5. Wrap two lengths of wire round the end of a paintbrush to create spirals.

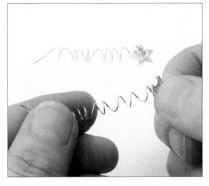

6. Thread a sequin star on to the end of each spiral and bend the wire ends back to secure them.

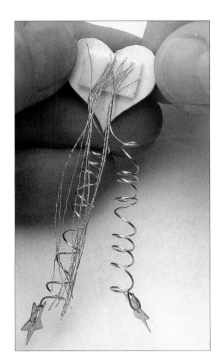

7. Lay the wires and some small lengths of gold thread on to the sticky pad.

8. Press the heart on to the star decoration.

9. Using the back of the scalpel, score the corrugated card down the middle, and fold.

10. Apply sticky pads to the back of the star (see inset) and press it on to the corrugated card.

11. Tie a length of gold cord round the fold, tying it in a bow at the top.

Choose festive outline stickers and rich colours to decorate your Christmas cards and presents. Add wire, ribbon and craft jewels for extra interest and sparkle.

Teddy Bear Box

Papier-mâché boxes are ideal to decorate with outline stickers. There are lots of box blanks in different shapes available. Take time to choose a shape to reflect your message or the occasion. This heart-shaped box has been decorated to hold a gift for a new baby. Sponging the acrylic paint on to the box gives an even, slightly textured surface – a perfect base for your sticker decoration.

You will need

- Silver outline stickers as shown
- Heart-shaped papier-mâché box blank
- Blue and cream acrylic paints
- Palette
- Blue card, 7 x 7cm (2¾ x 2¾in)
- Two 20cm (8in) lengths of blue ribbon
- Sponge
- Double-sided sticky pads
- Scalpel and cutting mat

The stickers used in this project.

1. Sponge the top of the lid with cream paint.

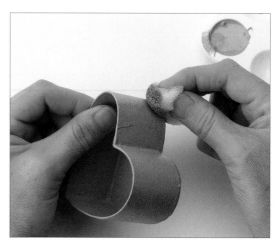

2. Sponge the base with blue paint.

3. Sponge the edge of the lid with blue paint, overlapping the top slightly to create a border. Leave to dry.

4. Apply the thin border sticker lines around the base, trimming the ends of the border with a scalpel to neaten it.

5. Run two border sticker lines round the edge of the lid.

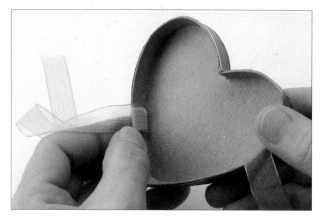

6. Stick a length of ribbon to the underside of each edge of the lid with sticky pads.

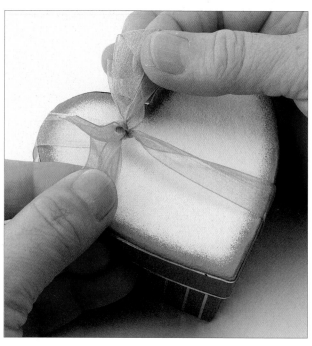

7. Tie the ribbon in a bow.

8. Press the teddy bear sticker on to blue card and cut round it with a scalpel.

9. Apply sticky pads to the back of the sticker and press it on to the lid.

Opposite:
The finished box is a perfect container for a special gift or memento.

Opposite:

Transform plain gift boxes with some paint and outline stickers. Make a card to match the box decoration for that special occasion.

The unusual shape of this wonderful box invites you to look inside – perfect for a suprise present.

Glitter Greetings Card

Now it is time to add some sparkle to your craftwork. As a lover of anything glitzy, I thoroughly enjoy demonstrating this technique. It really does transform the humble outline sticker. Using acetate as a base, the sticker is pressed on to the front and the glitter work is done on the back using clear glue. When the glue dries, you are left with a truly professional finish to your motif and it can then be mounted in a window card.

You will need

- Silver outline sticker as shown
- Pink card, 18 x 24cm (7 x 9½in)
- Acetate, 7 x 8cm (2¾ x 3in)
- Background paper, 7 x 8cm (2¾ x 3in)
- White glue fitted with a fine nozzle
- Pink and green fine glitter
- Soft paintbrush
- Pencil
- Ruler
- Ballpoint pen
- Scalpel and cutting mat
- Masking tape

The stickers used in this project.

The template for the Glitter Greetings Card, reproduced at half of the actual size. Enlarge it to 200 per cent on a photocopier.

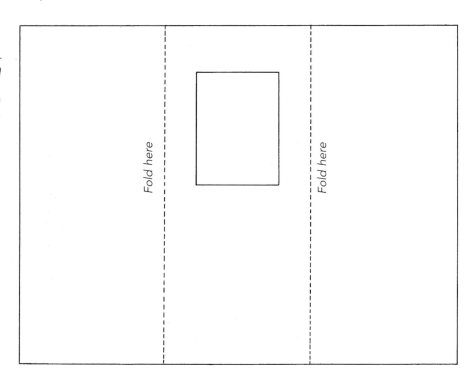

Fold here

Fold here

1. Lay your floral sticker on to a piece of acetate.

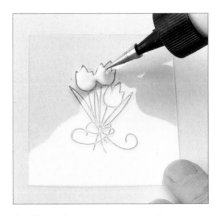

2. Turn the acetate over. Squeeze white glue over the petal sections.

3. Sprinkle with pink glitter.

4. Shake off any excess glitter and brush away any remaining particles with the paintbrush.

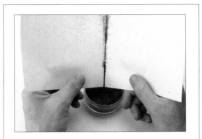

Tip

Sprinkle glitter over paper. When you have finished, you can pick up the paper and pour the excess back into the pot.

5. Repeating this process, decorate the leaves with green glitter. Leave to dry.

6. Score the pink card down the fold lines using the template to help you.

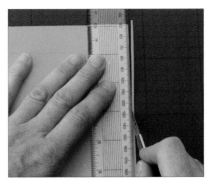

7. Cut a 2mm (¼in) strip from the right-hand edge.

8. Cut out the aperture in the middle card section and turn the card over.

9. Place the acetate design face down over the aperture and tape it into position with small pieces of masking tape.

10. Tape the background paper over the top.

Tip

Use spray adhesive in a well-ventilated area, and spray it into a box.

11. Lay a piece of scrap paper over the right-hand side and spray the left-hand flap with spray adhesive.

12. Fold the glued flap over.

13. Decorate the card with heart stickers.

This simple yet elegant design is brought to life by the sparkle and shine of the glitter and acetate.

Now you have mastered the art of applying glitter, look out for more complicated stickers to decorate. Traditional and classic designs work especially well. This butterfly picture demonstrates how simple ideas can be made to look both unusual and attractive.

Opposite:

As you can see, the Glitter Greetings Card is easily adapted for any occasion, from wedding anniversaries to 'get well soon' wishes.

Three-Dimensional Butterfly Picture

I expect many of you have had a go at three-dimensional papercraft, but did you know that outline stickers specifically designed for this purpose are available? You will find that all the motifs needed to create the design are printed on one outline sticker sheet, so all you will need is some coloured card, a sharp scalpel and a little patience. Choosing to back your design with a contrasting, darker-coloured card will really make the butterflies stand out.

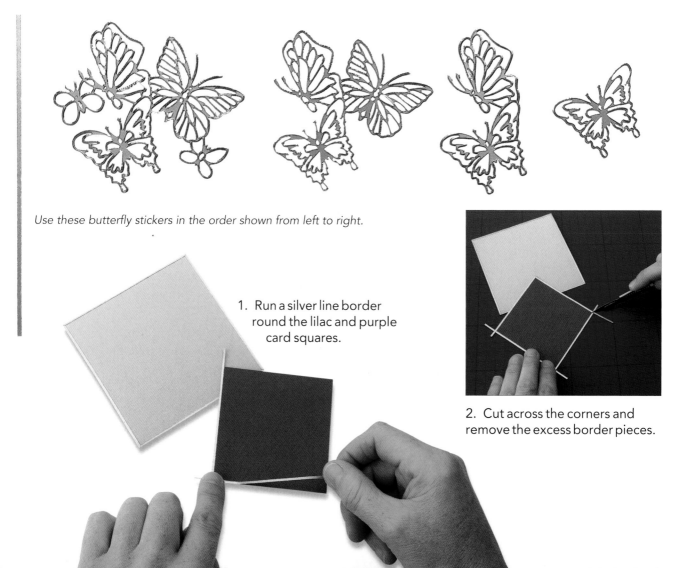

Use these butterfly stickers in the order shown from left to right.

1. Run a silver line border round the lilac and purple card squares.

2. Cut across the corners and remove the excess border pieces.

3. Glue the purple square to the middle of the lilac square with spray adhesive.

4. Press the outline stickers on to the A5 sheet of lilac card.

5. Cut around the stickers carefully.

Tip

Always have a sharp blade on your scalpel when cutting.

6. Apply sticky pads to the back of the butterflies.

7. Remove the backing papers and press the largest butterfly sticker on to the purple card square.

8. Press the second sticker in place on top of the first.

9. Press the third sticker on top of the second.

10. Press the final sticker on top of the third.

11. Mount your finished picture in the frame.

12. Decorate the frame with further butterfly stickers.

The finished Butterfly Picture. Decorating the frame with butterflies in this way brings the whole picture together.

Three-dimensional stickers come in lots of different designs. The stickers used here were pressed on to white card and coloured with paint or crayons before being cut out and mounted.

Christmas Decorations

Gold and silver outline stickers lend themselves perfectly to making Christmas decorations. By mounting them on to acetate and painting them with glass paints you really can give a jewel-like appearance to your creations. Hanging them in the window with the light shining through them will set them off perfectly. Apply the paint generously, to avoid brushmarks.

You will need

- Outline stickers as shown
- Acetate, 12 x 12cm (4¾ x 4¾in)
- Two 10 x 10cm (4 x 4in) sheets of pink card
- Pink glass paint
- Craft jewels
- Silver wire and old scissors
- Paintbrush
- Scalpel and cutting mat
- Pencil
- Ruler
- Spray adhesive
- Clear glue
- Hole cutting tool and mat
- Hammer

The stickers used in this project.

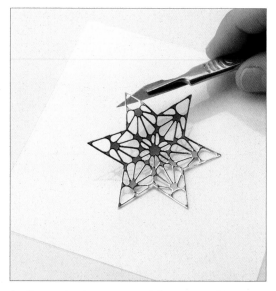

1. Press the large star sticker on to the acetate square.

2. Turn it over and paint the star with pink glass paint, applying the paint generously. Set aside to dry.

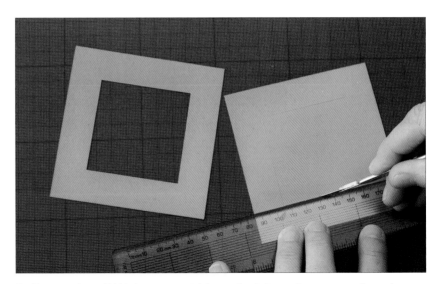

3. Draw a 6cm (2¼in) square within each pink card square and cut them out to make the card frames.

4. Coat the back of one of the pink card frames with spray adhesive. Press it on to the acetate so that the sticker is central.

5. Cut off the overhanging acetate and turn the design over.

6. Coat the back of the remaining card frame with spray adhesive and press it over the first.

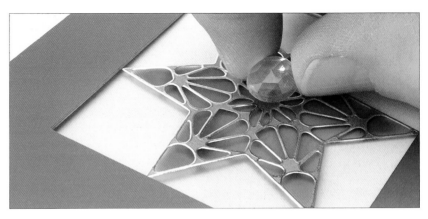

7. Glue a craft jewel to the middle of the star sticker using the clear glue.

8. Punch a hole in the top corner of the card using the hole cutting tool, mat and hammer.

9. Decorate the frame with sticker stars.

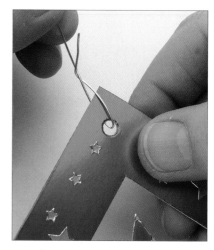

10. Cut a 12cm (4¾in) piece of wire using the old scissors. Secure this to the card frame through the hole at the top.

11. Wrap the middle section of wire round the end of a paintbrush to create a spiral.

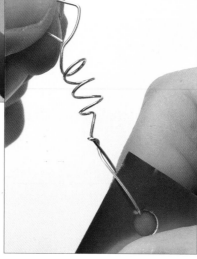

12. Make a hanging loop in the end and twist to secure.

13. Decorate the off-cut square of pink card with star stickers and a craft jewel, and attach a loop as for the main project.

Opposite:
These decorations look fantastic as part of a modern Christmas display.

*Don't just stick to square decorations.
Diamond-shaped card frames are
ideal for a more traditional feel to
your decorations – and remember to
decorate those off-cuts of card!*

Picture Frame

There is no need to go to great expense to create a picture frame. This one is made from thick card covered with handmade paper. Small heart stickers are used to create an all-over pattern, while painted outline stickers are used for additional interest around the aperture. You can adapt these instructions to create a frame of any shape or size.

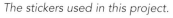

The stickers used in this project.

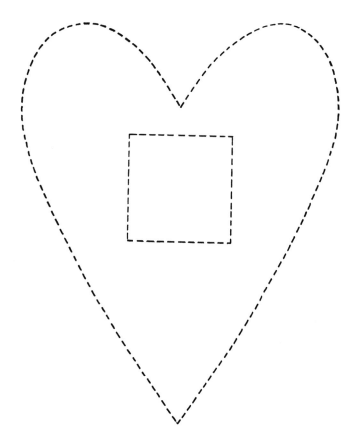

The template for the picture frame, reproduced at three quarters of the actual size. Enlarge it to 133 per cent on a photocopier.

You will need

- Outline stickers as shown
- Thick card, 14 x 16cm (5½ x 6¼in)
- Pink handmade paper
- White card, 10 x 15cm (4 x 6in)
- Mauve acrylic paint
- Paintbrush
- Mauve ribbon
- Spray adhesive
- Clear glue
- Double-sided sticky pads
- Pencil
- Ruler
- Scalpel and cutting mat
- Scissors

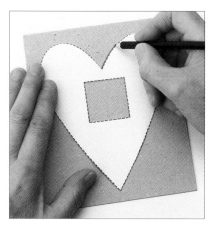

1. Photocopy the pattern, then cut it out and lay it on to the thick card. Draw round it with a pencil.

2. Cut out the card heart and aperture with a scalpel.

3. Cut a handmade paper heart 1cm (½in) larger than the pattern all round. Spray the back with spray adhesive. Press the card frame on to the middle of the paper.

4. Turn it over and smooth it flat.

5. Snip across the overhanging paper at the point of the heart. Cut a slit at the top (see inset).

6. Wrap the overhanging paper round on to the back of the frame.

7. Cut diagonally across the paper covering the aperture.

8. Fold the flaps over on to the back, trimming the top one.

9. Decorate the frame with small heart stickers.

10. Cut a slightly smaller heart shape from white card. Spread the back of the frame with clear glue. Press the white card heart on to the frame, trapping a loop of ribbon at the top (see inset).

11. Press the larger heart stickers on to white card. Paint them and cut them out.

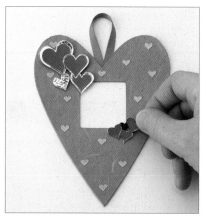

12. Apply sticky pads to the back of the heart decorations and press them on to your frame.

13. Glue a ribbon bow to the front.

14. Press a heart sticker on to handmade paper and tear around the edge. Apply spray adhesive to the back of the handmade paper and glue it to the aperture.

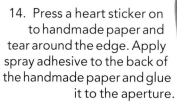

This heartfelt gift is perfect to surprise someone you love!

Inexpensive shop-bought frames are transformed with a little paint and some outline stickers.

Butterfly Book

I have used gold and silver outline stickers in the projects in this book. There are other colours on the market, but they are not so easily available. However, you will find marker pens specifically designed to colour the stickers and these are great fun to use. It adds a whole new dimension to your sticker projects as you can choose your own colour scheme for your projects. Here I have coloured the stickers with bright colours so that they will stand out against the orange and pink background papers.

You will need

- Outline stickers as shown
- Purple, orange and pink marker pens
- Notebook
- Orange handmade paper
- Double-sided sticky pads
- Spray adhesive
- Scalpel
- Cutting mat
- Round-ended scissors
- Pink card, 7 x 7cm (2¾ x 2¾in)
- Orange card, 7 x 8.5cm (2¾ x 3¼in)

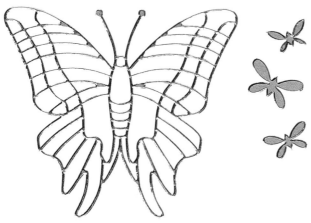

The stickers used in this project.

1. Cut a piece of orange handmade paper 2cm (¾in) larger than your opened notebook. Coat the back with spray adhesive and place your closed book on the right-hand side.

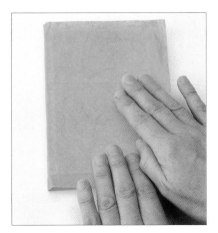

2. Wrap the paper round the closed book and smooth it flat.

3. Cut across the corners and then cut out a triangle either side of the spine at the top and bottom of the notebook.

4. Fold the overhanging paper to the inside of the book cover.

5. Open the cover, and using the point of a pair of scissors, push the two flaps inside the spine.

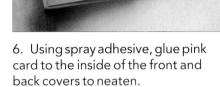

6. Using spray adhesive, glue pink card to the inside of the front and back covers to neaten.

Your book should now look like this.

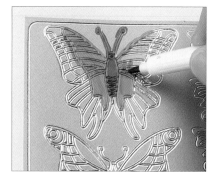

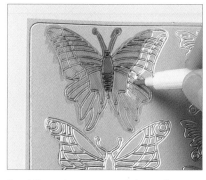

7. Colour the butterfly's body with the purple marker pen. Remember to do this while the sticker is still on the backing sheet.

8. Let the purple ink dry, then colour the inside of the butterfly's wings with the orange marker pen.

9. Allow the orange ink to dry, and then colour the rest of the wings with the pink marker pen.

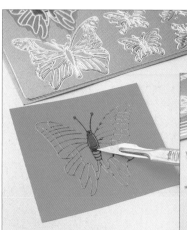

10. Peel the outline of the butterfly off the backing and press it on to the orange card. Carefully insert the small coloured segments of the butterfly's body.

11. Cut out the butterfly. Glue it to a 7cm (2¾in) square of pink card. Colour a border sticker pink and press it round the edge of the square. Trim the corners with a scalpel to neaten.

12. Apply sticky pads to the back of the square and press it on to the front of the notebook.

13. Colour smaller butterfly stickers with the orange and pink pens and decorate the cover with the butterflies.

This fabulous butterfly book is great for everything from keeping addresses to keeping secrets!

Use unusual and pretty coloured handmade papers to cover your books; this will really set off your coloured outline stickers.

Bookmark

We have decorated a book in the previous project, so how about making a bookmark to go with it? Outline stickers can be used very effectively to decorate metal foils. In this project I have also embossed the foil to give the design a three-dimensional feel. The finished embossed foil is then backed with card to strengthen it and to give an attractive border to the bookmark.

You will need

- Outline stickers as shown
- Thin gold embossing foil, 8 x 21cm (3 x 8¼in)
- Copper coloured card, 6 x 19cm (2¼ x 7½in)
- Gold ribbon
- Ballpoint pen
- Paintbrush
- Old notepad
- Clear adhesive
- Masking tape
- Ruler
- Scalpel and cutting mat
- Hole cutting tool and mat
- Hammer
- Cotton bud
- Craft jewels

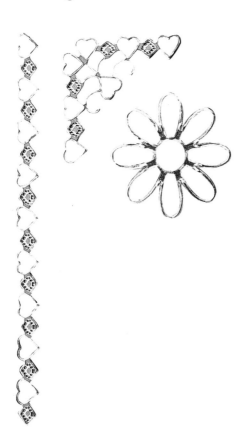

The stickers used in this project.

Tip

You can gently stretch border stickers to fit.

The template for the bookmark, reproduced at three quarters of the actual size. Enlarge it to 133 per cent on a photocopier.

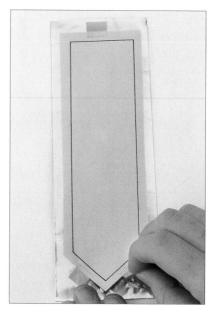

1. Photocopy the pattern, cut round it and tape it to the foil with masking tape.

2. Lay the foil on an old notepad. Use a ballpoint pen and ruler to trace the pattern on to the foil. Press firmly to achieve a good, strong line.

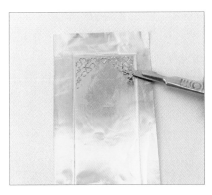

3. Remove the pattern. Press two corner stickers on to the top of the foil bookmark.

4. Press one corner sticker at the bottom of the bookmark.

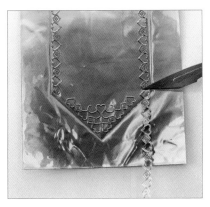

5. Run a border sticker down each side of the bookmark, trimming the end to fit.

6. Press four flower stickers down the middle of the bookmark.

7. Turn the foil over and, still working on the old notepad, gently rub the spaces in the outline stickers with a cotton bud to emboss the pattern on to the foil.

8. Emboss the hearts on the border with the rounded end of a paintbrush.

9. Emboss the flower petals in the same way.

10. Use a ballpoint pen to emboss a row of dots around the border.

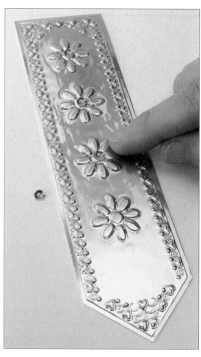

11. Cut out the foil bookmark on a cutting mat using a scalpel and ruler.

12. Spread clear glue over the back of the bookmark and press on to a piece of copper-coloured card. Cut round the card leaving a small border.

13. Glue a craft jewel to the centre of each flower.

14. Use the hole cutting tool, hammer and mat to punch a hole in the top of the bookmark.

15. Thread the gold ribbon through the hole, making a half-hitch as shown.

As well as looking fantastic, this bookmark is useful too.

Boxes and book covers can also be decorated with foil and outline stickers. More complicated corner motifs and borders are used to create a classic look to these bookmarks.

Mini Scrapbook

Scrapbooking is very popular at the moment, so here is an inexpensive way to create your own mini version. To give the scrapbook an aged appearance, the stickers are coloured with brown and pink marker pens and appropriate backing papers are used.

The stickers used in this project.

1. Cut out the rectangle of card for the scrapbook. Score it 10cm (4in) in from each short end using the back of the scalpel, and fold.

2. Turn the rectangle over. Measure and draw a line down the middle. Score using the back of the scalpel.

3. Fold your mini scrapbook into a concertina shape as shown.

4. Spray a 10cm (4in) square of the lighter backing paper with spray adhesive and press it on to the front of the scrapbook.

5. Cut a 3.5cm x 10cm (1½ x 4in) piece of darker background paper. Tear a 5mm (¼in) strip from the left-hand edge. Glue into place using spray adhesive.

6. Cut a 6.5cm (2½in) square of darker background paper. Tear 5mm (¼in) from each edge and glue the torn square to the scrapbook.

7. Colour the large heart in alternate stripes with the brown and pink pens. Leave the ink to dry for a few moments.

8. Press the large heart on to a piece of the dark background paper, then cut it out.

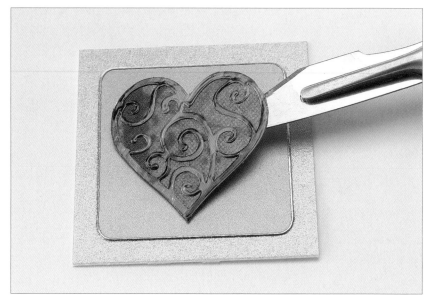

9. Press a gold square sticker on to the gold card and glue the heart to the centre.

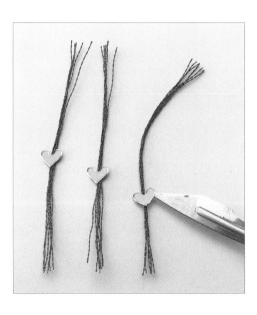

10. Cut three lengths of copper embroidery thread, each approximately 6.5cm (2½in). Press a small heart on to each length at varying heights.

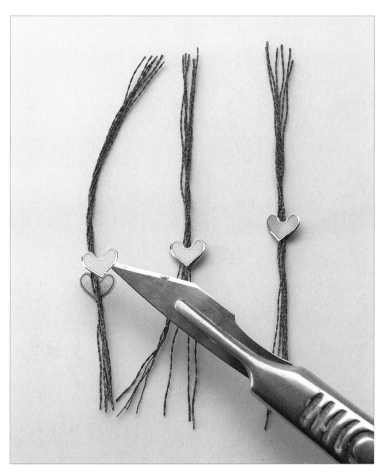

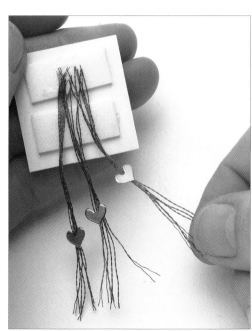

12. Apply sticky pads to the back of the decoration and lay the threads on the pads.

11. Turn the lengths of thread over and stick another small heart on to the back of each one.

13. Press the decoration on to the torn square.

14. Colour the small hearts in alternate stripes with the brown and pink pens.

15. Decorate the dark paper strip with the small coloured hearts.

This mini scrapbook would also make an unusual and imaginative Valentine's card. You can create a unique gift by decorating the scrapbook pages with photographs and mementos, or leave them blank for the recipient to fill.

This scrapbook has been decorated inside and out with a 'heritage' theme to give you ideas on how to decorate the inner pages of your scrapbook.

Opposite:
This scrapbook for a new baby shows how versatile these mini scrapbooks are. You can easily increase the size of the mini scrapbook template to make a larger version.

Scrapbook Page

Creating a scrapbook page gives you a wealth of opportunity to use outline border stickers. Use border, label and motif outline stickers to enhance your pictures. This project shows me enjoying the delights of the garden, so I have chosen floral borders, flowers and butterflies, all of which complement the theme.

You will need

- Outline stickers as shown
- Two photographs, 5 x 7cm (2 x 2¾in) and 7 x 14cm (2¾ x 5½in)
- Green card, 21 x 21cm (8¼ x 8¼in)
- Blue card, 20 x 20cm (8 x 8in)
- Lilac handmade paper, 10 x 19cm (4 x 7½in)
- Hole cutting tool and mat
- Hammer
- Raffia
- Spray adhesive
- Double-sided sticky pads
- Scalpel and cutting mat

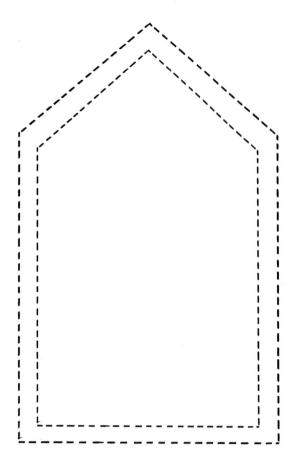

The template for the label, reproduced at full size. The outer dotted line is for the green label, the inner line for the blue label.

The stickers used in this project.

1. Glue the square of blue card to the middle of the square of green card and edge it with the floral border sticker.

2. Tear 5mm (¼in) from each edge of the handmade paper. Using spray adhesive, glue it to the right-hand side of the page.

3. Edge both photographs with the straight line border stickers and trim the ends.

4. Glue the larger photograph to the handmade paper panel.

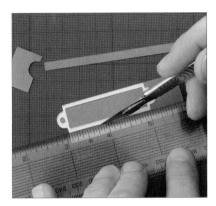

5. Press the gold label sticker to the green card and cut it out.

6. Glue the label decoration under the large photograph. Decorate it with flower stickers.

7. Photocopy the larger label template. Cut it out and trace round it on to green card. Cut out the label.

8. Cut a smaller blue label using the smaller template to help you. Glue it to the green label and edge it with the floral border sticker.

9. Glue the smaller photograph into place. Working on the mat, punch a hole at the top of the label using the hole cutting tool and hammer.

10. Press an eyelet sticker over the hole.

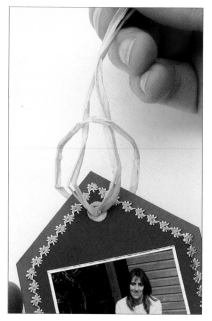

11. Fold a length of raffia in two and push the folded end through the hole. Pull the other ends through the loop to create a half-hitch as shown.

12. Tighten the raffia loop by pulling gently, and tie in a bow.

13. Attach the label to the page with sticky pads and then decorate the page with floral and butterfly stickers.

The finished scrapbook page. The colours and outline stickers used here work together with the photographs and show them in their best light.

Choose appropriate stickers to decorate your themed scrapbook pages.

Colours that complement the subject produce a really professional look.

Jewelled Box

A special gift needs a special box. The box used here was bought already coloured. Look for unusual colours to combine with your embellishments to set off your outline stickers. I have used a sticker sheet that contains a lot of small motifs for this project. When applied evenly to the box lid, they create a rich overall pattern – the perfect base for the jewel-like embellishments.

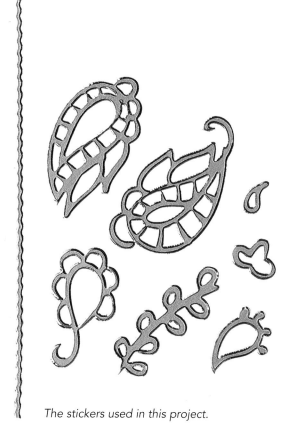

The stickers used in this project.

1. Press the decorative larger stickers over the lid of the box and fill in the spaces with small stickers.

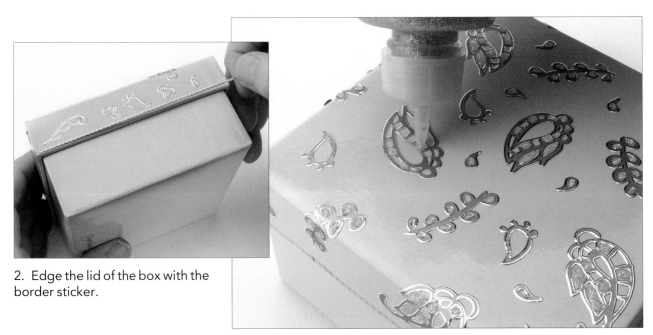

2. Edge the lid of the box with the border sticker.

3. Decorate the stickers with green glitter glue by filling in the smaller spaces in the motifs.

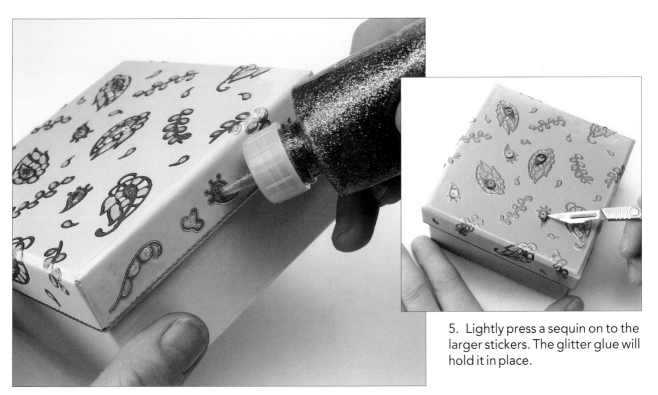

5. Lightly press a sequin on to the larger stickers. The glitter glue will hold it in place.

4. Fill in the centres of the larger motifs with pink glitter glue.

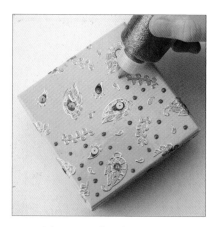

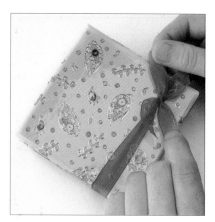

7. Wrap a pink ribbon around the box and the lid, then tie it in a bow on the top.

6. Add spots of pink glitter in between the stickers.

8. Decorate the matching gift tag in the same way.

The finished box could hold any number of exciting surprises!

This array of boxes shows how different each one can be made to look, just by decorating with stickers and craft jewels. Be as zany as you want with your colours and decorations. Have fun!

Index

This card was made using the embossing technique shown on pages 54–57.